A WIDENING LIGHT:
Poems
of the Incarnation

Luci Shaw, editor

Harold Shaw Publishers
Wheaton, Illinois

for Clyde & Martha

Copyright © 1984 by Luci Shaw

Printed in the United States of America

Design: Kathy Lay Burrows

Cover photo: Luci Shaw

ISBN 0-87788-930-9

Library of Congress Cataloging in Publication Data
Main entry under title:

A Widening light.

  (Wheaton literary series)
  1. Incarnation—Poetry. 2. Christian poetry,
American. 3. American poetry—20th century.
I. Shaw, Luci. II. Series.
PS595.I53W53 1984   811'.54'080382   84-13918
ISBN 0-87788-930-9

First printing, October 1984

Contents

First light

It is an early morning like all others.
The moonlight slants along the snow. Faint stars
Dissolve into the sky. The household,
Cat and children, deeply sleep.

It is a morning like no other morning.
There is a signifying in the silver dawn.
Stars hesitate, streets listen,
Snow melts in tenderness, trees wait.

The strangeness of the moment quiets lungs
and blood. The touching of a cup,
The turning of a page, is holy.
Even the stillness of the room breathes wonder.

Child, Light to my soul-shadow, my confusion,
Coming sweetly, and so small,
Growing within, a stealth, a mystery—
I am moved by this simplicity.

Transfixed with thanks, folded in love,
I cannot adore enough. I cannot speak.
Like trees and snow and stars and street,
I too am silent in the widening light.

Myrna Reid Grant

A quintina of crosses

Beyond, beneath, within, wherever blood,
If there were blood, flows with the pulse of love,
Where God's circle and all orbits cross,
Through the black space of death to baby life
Came God, planting the secret genes of God.

By the permission of a maiden's love,
Love came upon the seeds of words, broke blood,
And howled into the Palestine of life,
A baby roiled by memories of God.
Sometimes he smiled, sometimes the child was cross.

Often at night he dreamed a dream of God
And was the dream he dreamed. Often across
The lily fields he raged and lived their life,
And heaven's poison festered in his blood,
Loosing the passion of unthinkable love.

But mostly, though, he lived a prentice's life
Until a singing in the surge of blood,
Making a chorus of the genes of God,
Flailed him into the tempest of a love
That lashed the North Star and the Southern Cross.

His neighbors smelled an alien in his blood,
A secret enemy and double life;
He was a mutant on an obscene cross
Outraging decency with naked love.
He stripped the last rags from a proper God.

The life of God must blood this cross for love.

Chad Walsh

Annunciation

The sun erupts   windows frame
a cold blue sea
a breeze feathers her untucked hair as
she leaves her lean to
finish sweeping
under worn mats   old painted chairs

in a start   she stops
sees her shadow shorten

an angel's face grows
wide in delight
"Rejoice   you   so highly favored
your womb shall seed promised land and
sky."

With one hand behind her she
backs through her mind

She listens
peace finds peace
"Yes." leaves her room   and its filling

the grey table sways
her heart follows her down
last leaf to the ground
fall   colors   every girlish way.

David Craig

Too much to ask

it seemed too much to ask
of one small virgin
that she should stake shame
against the will of God.
all she had to hold to
were those soft, inward
flutterings
and the remembered sting
of a brief junction—spirit
with flesh.
who would think it
more than a dream wish?
an implausible, laughable
defence.

and it seems much
too much to ask me
to be part of the
different thing—
God's shocking, unorthodox,
unheard of Thing
to further heaven's hopes
and summon God's glory.

Luci Shaw

Christmas dream

". . . an angel of the Lord appeared to him in a dream."
Matthew 1:20

Amiably at home with virtue and evil—
the righteousness of Joseph and Herod's
wickedness—I'm ever and always a stranger to grace.
I need this annual angel visitation

—this sudden dive by dream into reality—
to know the virgin conceives and God is with us.
The dream powers its way through winter weather
and gives me vision to see the Jesus gift.

Light from the dream lasts a year. Through
equinox and solstice I am given twelve months

of daylight by which to build the crêche where my
Redeemer lives. The fetus of praise grows

deep in my spirit. As autumn wanes I count
the days until I bear the dream again.

Eugene H. Peterson

Christmas Eve, Jerusalem Road

The fir tree is filled
with tin trefoils
and a rosary of winking
white lights.
One weather-greyed window inhaling
the darkness will do, for now
I am layered in Advent.
Faces are watching me
from a hundred glass balls—our mouths
all crease and break
into colored round teeth.

If you were here we'd be touching
the gifts, touching each other,
watching the bulbs' soundless popping
brighten the night.
But now I wait and wait.
I am the lone center of this tinsel
universe, flying cloudlike
in and out of a needle
nebula and its knots of light.
My eyes are full of stars.

*   *   *

Suddenly, your high & low throats,
soon nearing, spin yarn
from the empty air.
My silence is threaded as wind
spills through the door
like hope

and Jesus begs
to be born.

Kelli Conlin

The risk of birth

This is no time for a child to be born,
With the earth betrayed by war & hate
And a nova lighting the sky to warn
That time runs out & the sun burns late.

That was no time for a child to be born,
In a land in the crushing grip of Rome;
Honour & truth were trampled by scorn—
Yet here did the Saviour make his home.

When is the time for love to be born?
The inn is full on the planet earth,
And by greed & pride the sky is torn—
Yet Love still takes the risk of birth.

Madeleine L'Engle

After annunciation

This is the irrational season
When love blooms bright and wild.
Had Mary been filled with reason
There'd have been no room for the child.

Madeleine L'Engle

Housekeeper

This is my little town,
My Bethlehem,
And here, if anywhere,
My Christ Child
Will be born.

I must begin
To go about my day—
Sweep out the inn,
Get fresh hay for the manger
And be sure
To leave my heart ajar
In case there may be travelers
From afar.

Elizabeth Rooney

Advent

Shepherds, donkeys, comets, kings . . .
This year I ponder private things:
How Mary, innocent and poor,
Felt carrying a baby prince
Inside, until she bore
Him whimpering. I wonder, since
This Christmas I am filled
With my firstborn to carry . . .
And when the wind is stilled
At night I think of Mary.

Margaret D. Smith

Hewn hands

Little Mary
she's a buried cargo
wrapped in so many blankets I
    have to smile
she reminds me of the circus fat
    lady
who sweats   chin over chin
while the donkey bears in silence
his retribution

at the hotel
a drunk swings out a second story
    window
it was two in the morning as he sang
to the cheering crowd below
Is it so much to ask for?
some clean floor to have our son
is it so much to ask for?
a room for a beggar and his family

Mary muffles her time
Lord God it is her time!
shall we have Your Son on the side
    of the road
invite the beasts of the field
every straggler   every all-night
    pilgrim?

David Craig

Birth of our Lord

Spring was breaking through the ground
sheep   in the hills   stumbled over
  melting snow
homing in on grassy mounds

In the cave the straw was cold
and snapped sounding
each time her body rolled

Joseph scattered the chickens
ran his fingers deep in the straw
working the ends
He arranged his cloak   her nest

at the mouth of the cave he stretched
but below the town   the hills   light
he heard people at windows
on the streets   pointing   he looked
up and shrank beneath a blaze of light

Mary puffed in the cool of night air
silently contracted
her fingers   the carpenter's shoulder

Jesus

His hair   curly   black
eyes closed
His thin legs kicked as Joseph
placed Him in Mary's arms
sheep and angels sang
Hills   palms   brought visitors   gifts

David Craig

Advice for the calendar

The first snow should not fall on Christmas, not
On any of its twelve green indoor feast days, but
In difficult, rude mid-winter when the last
Fir tree, in its false rain dangerously dry, is cast
Outdoors with the trash and all warm Christmas seems,
Perhaps, like rubbish to us in our cold extremes
Looking back from among the insults of the ordinary year.
In actual winter, the wind true north, at the unclear
Removal of the sun from the sky—if it snow first then,
We may feast once more and drink to the health of men
In the pure Christ coming gently to earth again.
The first snow, raising a little the lowly lay
Of our land, soothing our streets at wintertide,
In general softening the blow of winter, should not
   coincide
With Christmas. It itself is a holy day.

Jene Beardsley

" . . . for who can endure the day of his coming?"
Malachi 3:2

When an angel
   snapped the old thin threads of speech
      with an untimely birth
   announcement, slit
   the seemly cloth of an even
      more blessed event with the
   shears of miracle,
   invaded the privacy of a dream,
multiplied
   to ravage the dark silk of the sky, the
      innocent ears
   with swords of sound:
news in a new dimension demanded
   qualification.
The righteous were as vulnerable as others.
   they trembled for those strong
   antecedent *fear nots,* whether goat-
      herds, virgins, workers in wood or
         holy barren priests.

In our nights our
   complicated modern dreams rarely
      flower into visions. No
      contemporary Gabriel
   dumbfounds our worship, or burning,
   visits our bedrooms. No
sign-post satellite hauls us, earth-bound but
star-struck, half
   around the world with hope.

Are our sensibilities
   too blunt to be assaulted
      with spatial power-plays and far-out
   proclamations of peace? Sterile,
skeptics, yet we may be broken
      to his slow silent birth
      (new-torn, new-
       born ourselves at his
        beginning new in us).
His bigness may still burst
     out self-containment
   to tell us—without angels' mouths—
fear not.

God knows we need to hear it, now
      when he may shatter
     with his most shocking coming
   this proud cracked place
and more if, for longer waiting,
      he does not.

Luci Shaw

Anno Domini, 1980

There's straw in my hat from a weekend hayride,
and new sweet straw for the rabbit hutches.
My mind wanders as I coil a wreath for a holiday doorway
and think of a child being born on straw in a stable.
The prime rate this week is 21%; we buy less than last.
We are not poor by any man's measure, but then a carpenter
borrowed a donkey for the census-taking trip,
a lonely, heavy journey for newlyweds
married under rather extraordinary terms.
If they were anxious—bills due, a child on the way—
the record says little of that.
Just that the city was overcrowded—nothing new—
and there were no rooms left.
We can identify: all of us journeymen,
preoccupied, bewildered, looking for prophets—
this is an era of cults, the Word in disguise so often
we cannot tell who is hustling whom.
But the stargazing countrymen heard the news,
or heard it true before the rest.
"God. God is with us," having hillsides of time
    to look up at the sky.

Nancy Nase Thomas

O Sapientia

It was from Joseph first I learned
Of love. Like me he was dismayed.
How easily he could have turned
Me from his house; but, unafraid,
He put me not away from him
(O God-sent angel, pray for him).
Thus through his love was Love obeyed.

The Child's first cry came like a bell:
God's Word aloud, God's Word in deed.
The angel spoke: so it befell,
And Joseph with me in my need.
O Child whose father came from heaven,
To you another gift was given,
Your earthly father chosen well.

With Joseph I was always warmed
And cherished. Even in the stable
I knew that I would not be harmed.
And, though above the angels swarmed,
Man's love it was that made me able
To bear God's Love, wild, formidable,
To bear God's Will, through me performed.

Madeleine L'Engle

Shine in the dark

I   From a dark dust of stars
kindled one, a prick of light.
Burn! small candle star,
burn in the black night.
In the still hushed heart
(dark as a black night)
shine! Savior newly born,
shine, till the heart's light!

II   Into blackness breached with white
the star shivers like a bell.
God of birth and brightness
bless the cool carillon
singing into sight!
Plot its poised pointing flight!
Dark has its victories
tonight, in David's town.
But the star bell's tongue
trembles silver still
in your felicity.

III   The stars look out on
roofs of snow.
They see the night,
a velvet glow
with amber lanterns
shining so.
God searches through
the sweep of night.
Is there a heart burns
warm and bright
to warm God's own heart
at the sight?

Luci Shaw

Night's lodging

Across the purple-patterned snow
laced with light of lantern-glow,
dappled with dark,
comes Christ, the Child born from the skies.
Those are stars that are his eyes.
His baby face is wise
seen by my candle spark.
But is he cold from the wind's cold blow?
Where will he go?

I'll wrap him warm with love,
well as I'm able,
in my heart stable.

Luci Shaw

At Christ's birth

a small bird
bore up rafters
on its wings

a weanling calf
settled
in the straw

there was a sound
almost impossible
as fontanel
parting crystal

Sandra R. Duguid

Judah's Lion

Where does the lion, Judah's golden lion walk?
Stealthy under star by winter night his soft paws stalk.
Out on lonely hills a cold wind howls and darkness scowls;
Shepherds shiver—danger in the dark!—some wild beast prowls.
Suddenly up springs a light; a voice rings like a bell:
"Joy, O men of Judah! Come and see! Noel! Noel!"
Where lies Judah's longed-for lion? "Come and see the sight!
Fear not—your golden one is couched among the lambs tonight."

Keith Patman

Lion, Lamb

The sleepless child,
thunder approaching
and then the claws clicking
and scraping at the window.
On the stairs the padding
of enormous paws, the slow breath
in her neck. Even in daytime
she fears the eyes, golden
in the sky.

This same kingly force
held in a lamb?
Incomprehensible. Absurd.
Power concealed in somersaults,
in this bleating-after-me
for the milk of my affections?
Strength laid down
so that I, child-woman,
may clutch this dumb, damp,
reckless, woolly thing
against my thumping heart?

Jean Janzen

Like every newborn

Like every newborn, he has come from very far.
His eyes are closed against the brilliance of the star.
So glorious is he, he goes to this immoderate length
To show his love for us, discarding power and strength.
Girded for war, humility his mighty dress,
He moves into the battle wholly weaponless.

Madeleine L'Engle

Truer gifts

The whole world (it seems)
is soaring into Christmas
meeting the cold with such proper spirit
hanging up pines with bulbs and best wishes,
meaningless to minds set in tradition
and premature weariness for celebrating routine.
(I never understood it either):

Being fond of dolls then
I got a new one every year
packaged in paper and parent-love.
I ripped away wrappings
and months of anticipation
to touch my own just born babies,
more real than any mangered child
mysteriously coming in the very olden days.
They cried faucet water tears
(not salty but still strong)
I laughed at their damp faces
sometimes.
No one ever told me that santa made money
by stuffing himself in a red rented suit
or that the cookies I left hot for him
were munched by the dog
as I buried my head in a pillow
white with dreams.

It always ended too soon:
hopes flickered away as colored lights blinked
    into black
brittle needles left trails behind the retreating tree
and the nativity surrendered the TV top to magazines.
Songs fled the streets and people forgot to smile
snow melted
and dolls lay broken on a closet shelf.

I shall make no neat list this year
(carefully itemized from Sears' catalog);
needing nothing in the way of plastic infants
I ask for truer gifts:
that I might glow sharper than any tinselled star
showing God's good love to every innkeeper
and all astonished shepherds.

Lisa Leafstrand

God given

Christmas means gifts.
In the wide, wheeling universe
There has been only one—
One gift once given,
One infinite, eternal, perfect joy—
One baby boy.

Elizabeth Rooney

O Simplicitas

An angel came to me
And I was unprepared
To be what God was using.
Mother I was to be.
A moment I despaired,
Thought briefly of refusing.
The angel knew I heard.
According to God's Word
I bowed to this strange choosing.

A palace should have been
The birthplace of a king
(I had no way of knowing).
We went to Bethlehem;
It was so strange a thing.
The wind was cold, and blowing,
My cloak was old, and thin.
They turned us from the inn;
The town was overflowing.

God's Word, a child so small,
Who still must learn to speak,
Lay in humiliation.
Joseph stood, strong and tall.
The beasts were warm and meek
And moved with hesitation.
The Child born in a stall?
I understood it: all.
Kings came in adoration.

Perhaps it was absurd:
A stable set apart,
The sleepy cattle lowing;
And the incarnate Word
Resting against my heart.
My joy was overflowing.
The shepherds came, adored
The folly of the Lord,
Wiser than all men's knowing.

Madeleine L'Engle

Star witness

How could we be anything but true
    believers—
We shepherds who heard the news
    first-hand from Heaven!

There stood that angel on the
    grazing-ground
Like a white fan,
Like a white blaze,
    lighting the air all around;
Telling us the Promised One had come,
And where He was,
And what His destiny.

And then that great arc of angels
Singing a gloria.

We left our sheep that night
And found the Lamb.

Beth Merizon

God tries on skin

Once, he stretched skin over spirit
like a rubber glove,
aligning trinity with bone,
twining through veins
until deity square-knotted flesh.

In a whirlwind spin
he shrank to the size of a zygote,
bobbed in a womb warm as Galilee's shore.

In the dark,
he brushed up on Hebrew,
practiced his crawl.

After months scrunched in a circle,
he burst through his cellophane sac,
bloodied the teen legs
spread on the straw.

In his first breath
he inhaled the sweat
of Romans casting lots,
sniffed the wine mixed with gall.

Marjorie Maddox Phifer

Made flesh

After the bright beam of hot annunciation
fused heaven with dark earth
his searing sharply-focused light
went out for a while
eclipsed in amniotic gloom:
his cool immensity of splendor
his universal grace
small-folded in a warm dim
female space—
the Word stern-sentenced
to be nine months dumb—
infinity walled in a womb
until the next enormity—the Mighty,
after submission to a woman's pains
helpless on a barn-bare floor
first-tasting bitter earth.

Now, I in him surrender
to the crush and cry of birth.
Because eternity
was closeted in time
he is my open door
to forever.
From his imprisonment my freedoms grow,
find wings.
Part of his body, I transcend this flesh.
From his sweet silence my mouth sings.
Out of his dark I glow.
My life, as his,
slips through death's mesh,
time's bars,
joins hands with heaven,
speaks with stars.

Luci Shaw

Christmas program

Now the world
is clean as ice,
starlight chinks
on the schoolroom pane,
children whisper
through the scent of pine,
wet wool and oranges.

They tell the story.
Their voices
are strings and horns.
They are braiding
a cord to hold
and pass on
in the long night.

We are in the stable
sheltered from
the prairie wind.
The tree is fresh as our love.
We stand breathless
for the lighting
of the wicks.
As the fire spreads,
we melt like wax.

Jean Janzen

Prayer at the Advent log

The small lights steady
against the dark,
Your flame touching ours.
Today is the fifth day.
It is a safe fire,
the candles still tall
above the brittle wood
of the birch, the air
damp and chill.
But the days will draw us
inexorably toward
Your celebration,
and again we'll stand
in the crackling air,
the first days' flames
licking the log
with their shortened lives,
the length of it
threatened by Your fire,
Your love dazzling our eyes,
and, O Christ,
Your light searing
our nakedness.

Jean Janzen

The Nativity

Among the oxen (like an ox I'm slow)
I see a glory in the stable grow
Which, with the ox's dullness might at length
   Give me an ox's strength.

Among the asses (stubborn I as they)
I see my Saviour where I looked for hay;
So may my beastlike folly learn at least
   The patience of a beast.

Among the sheep (I like a sheep have strayed)
I watch the manger where my Lord is laid;
Oh that my baa-ing nature would win thence
   Some wooly innocence!

C. S. Lewis

Some Christmas stars

Blazes the star behind the hill.
Snow stars glint from the wooden sill.
A spider spins her silver still

within Your darkened stable shed:
in asterisks her webs are spread
to ornament your manger bed.

Where does a spider find the skill
to sew a star? Invisible,
obedient, she works Your will

with her swift silences of thread.
I weave star-poems in my head;
the spider, wordless, spins instead.

Luci Shaw

The groundhog

The goundhog is, at best, a simple soul
   without pretension, happy in his hole,
twinkle-eyed, shy, earthy, coarse-coated grey,
   no use at all (except on Groundhog Day).
At Christmastime, a rather doubtful fable
   gives the beast standing room inside the stable
with other simple things, shepherds, and sheep,
   cows, and small winter birds, and on the heap
of warm, sun-sweetened hay, the simplest thing
   of all—a baby. Can a groundhog sing,
or only grunt his wonder? Could he know
   this new-born Child had planned *him*, long ago,
for groundhog-hood? Whether true tale or fable,
   I like to think that he *was* in the stable,
part of the Plan, and that He who designed
   all simple wonderers, may have had me in mind.

Luci Shaw

Child

Dear child, sweet child,
Sleeping in the straw,
We who come to worship you
Kneel now in awe.

Dear child, sweet child,
Sheltered in a stable,
Each of us would bring you
Gifts, as we are able.

Dear child, sweet child,
Lighted by a star,
Help our hearts to find you
No matter where we are.

Dear child, sweet child,
Willing to be man,
Teach us how to love you.
No one else can.

Elizabeth Rooney

In memory of Thomas Hardy

"While I watch the Christmas blaze
Paint the room with ruddy rays,
Something makes my vision glide
To the frosty scene outside."

". . . lo, I am with you always, even unto the end of the world."
Matthew 28:20

Beyond the wet black hole wiped into the
      windowfrost,
A bloodless thermometer predicts a difficult winter.
Here, in one reddening room, in the human face
      uncrossed
From its usual pain, the lights that flick and
      splinter
From the tree, the Christmas brandy, strong fire and
      laughter,
The small-berried holly hammocked over and under
      the rafter,
Far from the shag of murk-witted beasts and the
      field's crude straw,
The antique manger is restored to a modern finish.

The weather lows at tightly shut windows from
      kitchen to den.
It blows from a year before Rome made Christ law.
When did Christ's stable begin to look inn-ish
And rest us merry gentlemen?
Who find again Christ where we have always
      found him:

On the vacuumed pasture of the level rug, near the
    dawn-red blinds on the dimmer
Window, in our own kind dress where it is always
    summer,
The swaddling clothes in which the known world
    has always bound him.

Outdoors, where cold burrs tug in the streetlit
    trees and the Pleistocene
North sky swells with storm, hung with icicles
    for terror
The roof like an omission sign points to our error,
To all that our cheer prefers not seen:
The sharp ice forming in the stratosphere, the lunar
    theaters where Christ draws no crowds,
Reeling Andromeda, the doubtful Magellanic clouds,
And all the silent dark light years unstrung between.

Jene Beardsley

This Christmas

we must know Him differently—
as though a bell rose
from the baby's face.

The tale of miracle is not enough,
nor are softly countenanced figurines
bedded down in imported straw
by fountain centers of outlying malls.

It must be written again;
physician Luke's story of beauty
however musical or true
is too distant and plain.

We must see all our ingenuities of metal
rising composite from flesh
as though our weapons have been redeemed.

We must hear in sirens
fallen petals.
Think, there are other ways it could mean.

Sandra R. Duguid

Away in a manger

"The little Lord Jesus
No crying He makes."
Bah Humbug.

True God made babe
bewails the warm womb lost;
hungry, screams and gropes for mother-milk.

True God made child
wants will his own;
in tears surrenders to another.

True God made man
weeps bitterly for friend death stole,
sobs silently at Simon's loud rejection.

True God made Christ
in blood-sweat groans
that cup be taken from him.

On cruel cross
with throat dry cries
asks why Good God has Son forsaken.

Barbara K. Olson

Snow

Was it a cold awakening Christmas morning
In a wooden trough,
In spite of straw and swaddling clothes and angel songs?
That was not to be the last time
You'd be laid upon the wood
(There were Herods, Judases from the start
Among the stars and shepherds).
And did they smile, those simple folk,
And kiss your tiny hands and weep delight?
They'd touch those hands again someday,
Believing you through cracks and scars.
   Then oh! the million Christmas mornings
When you'd lie, a babe again,
Beneath a million million trees
And hear the countless tongues chanting your name.
   And oh! the white snow on black shingles
Where icy crystals capture windows
And fires glow and mistletoe is wreathed and strung.
   But ah.... will they remember crimson
Dripping from the iron nails
And will they pray, and will they know
A whiter white than
   Snow?

Keith Patman

Mary's song

Blue homespun and the bend of my breast
keep warm this small hot naked star
fallen to my arms. (Rest . . .
you who have had so far
to come.) Now nearness satisfies
the body of God sweetly. Quiet he lies
whose vigor hurled
a universe. He sleeps
whose eyelids have not closed before.
His breath (so slight it seems
no breath at all) once ruffled the dark deeps
to sprout a world.
Charmed by doves' voices, the whisper of straw,
he dreams,
hearing no music from his other spheres.
Breath, mouth, ears, eyes
he is curtailed
who overflowed all skies,
all years.
Older than eternity, now he
is new. Now native to earth as I am, nailed
to my poor planet, caught that I might be free,
blind in my womb to know my darkness ended,
brought to this birth
for me to be new-born,
and for him to see me mended
I must see him torn.

Luci Shaw

"Thou didst make me hope upon my mother's breasts."
Psalm 22:9

Why are your eyes so far away,
   Little one, little one?
What are your lips shaped to say,
   My son, my son?

A breast for your lips and milk for your need,
   I offer my little one.
But where do your eyes steadily feed,
   Jesus, my little son?

The sun in the sky, a fleece of a cloud,
   I see, and my little one,
And a lark sings soft, and my heart sings loud
   To carol a newborn son.

Take what I have, the milk and the breast,
   Close your eyes, little one.
See when you must, but sleep is best,
   This hour, Jesus my son.

Chad Walsh

Rich man

Rich man, rich man, who are you?
Do you seek the Christ Child, too?
In your palace and your court,
Life is busy, life is short.
Have you time to go away
To find a baby in the hay?
Can you get your camel through
The needle's eye, as you must do?

Rich man, rich man, you've come far.
Where did you learn to trust a star
Instead of turning to a king
To guide you in your wandering?
Rich man, how did you grow wise
In spite of all your kingly guise?
Who taught you to play your part,
To bring an educated heart
To the stable in the west
So you could kneel there and be blessed?

Elizabeth Rooney

A maze of the Magi

Lord
We come
Through buyers bundle-bent
We never meant . . .

We carved our names
On bridges
Built by Currier and Ives
"Over the river and through the woods"
(The sleigh never arrives)

We flattered father's daughters
Mirroring
Holiday frocks:
Stoics disregarding
Their abundant cookie crocks

We combed through tinsel forests
Tangling
In artificial lights
Tracing nothing so electric
As the vacuum of your nights . . .

And we say
We have not found
Him paled
In a small nest

Magi

Even Magi

Come slowly

At best

Sandra R. Duguid

Star song

We have been having
epiphanies, like suns,
all this year long.
And now, at its close
when the planets
are shining through frost,
light runs like music
in the bones,
and the heart keeps rising
at the sound of any song.
An old magic flows
in the silver calling
of a bell,
rounding
high and clear,
flying, falling,
sounding
the death knell
of our old year,
telling the new appearing
of Christ, our Morning Star.

Now burst,
all our bell throats!
Toll,
every clapper tongue!
Stun the still night.
Jesus himself gleams through
our high heart notes
(it is no fable).
It is he whose light
glistens in each song sung
and in the true
coming together again
to the stable,

of all of us: shepherds,
sages, his women and men,
common and faithful,
wealthy and wise,
with carillon hearts
and suddenly, stars in our eyes.

Luci Shaw

The crystal hexagon

Out of the cloud a bright
    rosette;
Out of the void, form.
Space and line,
A frost design
Tumbles from the storm.

Out of the timeless
    into time;
From pure spirit, clay.
Out of the night
Imperial light—
The light, the truth,
    the way.

Beth Merizon

Christ-hymn

O You!
You tiny who
Of Simeons song
You shepherds shock
You singular star-bright

You student
Shunning company
And travel
For scholars light.

Just apprentice
Of your mothers husband
True measurer
And leveler
And line

Authoritative voice
Enlisting aid
Selector
And selected
And Divine.

Creative host
Of weddings, picnics, graves
Most social
And uncelebrated
Friend

You thoughtful martyr
You thirsty man
You dying God—

I hoped!
But this concludes . . .
                    Amen. Amen.

O
Heir of power
Crasher
Of closed meetings
The unsummoned
Inviting inspection—

You natural!
You Master
Of surprise.

Sandra R. Duguid

First parting
Luke 2:41-51

Our son! My God, in all this throng
not one that answers to his name.
He is not among our kin
nor has he tarried with our friends.
Him whom we love, our firstborn, is gone.

Like salmon, returning to our spawning place
we swim against the current
of the homeward-going crowds.
The feast is over, and Jerusalem
has closed in upon itself once more.

Deep shadowy streets
echo our anxious steps
as in a fitful dream.
Where could he be? Who
may have taken him from me? How dare he
treat us so? I weep in my heart
at this, our first parting.

A circle of the wise huddles in the temple.
But whose young head shines up in their midst?
What youth is this whose answers turn the old
to babbling babes again? Is this our son?

Joseph, Joseph, hold me close.
Close up this tear that has already started
the shredding of my heart.

Our son, our firstborn, though we have found him,
is gone.

Ruth El Saffar

Who was also himself looking
for the kingdom of God

The Jesus we have never known
(Come to think of it)
Is Jesus the boy,
Before he was twelve
And after he was twelve, you know.
What do we not know
(And want to know not for curiosity now)
Of Jesus in his twenties—
If folk in his village counted years by tens—
Or did they count by fives or twos or sevens,
Or not at all?
At twenty-one did he still think like a child
And form himself in his Galilean mind
Still a boy of eleven
(Which for boys is the best age)?

Lord, will we ever know you as a boy?
(Don't think we ask idly to interrupt your work
Of intercession day and night for the uttermost,
Just to peer at the missing things,
Like Pindar's other odes
Or all those epics Henry burned or left for Cromwell)
Will you be a boy for us someday?
Can you do it—and not as a phantasm,
But as you really were?
Or are you old, Lord, perpetually old,
Old as the Father, begotten from eternity?
Such abstractions block my starting joy,
Though they root and church me week by week, I'm told.

How old should we expect you to be
When we see you in heaven?
Jesus, don't just say you will be ageless
(Age matters lots to a boy, remember?)

Or whatever age we would like you to be
(Don't play Santa Claus with us, Lord).
Is it heretical of me to ask you once again
To be eleven?
Or did Pilate's seal on Joseph's tomb
Keep you always thirty-three?

Joe McClatchey

Creator

Jesus, Jesus,
Carpenter of Nazareth,
Can you make a lintel?
Can you make a door?

Jesus, Jesus,
Carpenter of Nazareth,
Can you make a universe
Where there was none before?

Jesus, Jesus,
Carpenter of Nazareth,
Living in the midst of us,
A working man and poor,

How shall we esteem you,
Holy, humble carpenter?
By the universe you made—
And also by the door.

Elizabeth Rooney

Craftsman

Did Jesus like
To be a carpenter,
Enjoy the smell of wood,
Laugh at the shavings
Curling from his plane?
Did he like sawdust
And the heft of tools,
Thrill at the feel
Of satin-polished grain?
And did he look
At things that he had made
And see that they were good
And glory in creating
Once again?

Elizabeth Rooney

Chance

Did God take his chances
on a son sent to fill flesh?
Was such metamorphosis
a divine risk?

Once embodied
might he not find
earth's poignancies too sharp,
sweet flesh too sweet
to soon discard?
Might not man's joys
   (the growing
   of body, mind and will,
   knowing
   companionship,
   the taste of shared bread,
   the smell of olives
   new-carved wood, and wine,
   morning's chill
   on a bare head,
   rough warm wool,
   a near, dust-blue Judean hill,
   evening's shine
   of oil lamps through an
   open door,
   day's work, tired muscles
   a bed on the floor)
make up for his limitations?
Might he not even
wish for a peaceful death
from old age?

Ah, Father, but you knew
the incarnation was no gamble!
We are the risk you run.

Our destiny is not so clearly defined.
It's either/or for us.

And when I say you took no chance
on him,
he being our one chance of heaven,
I mean rather
once chosen, he's no chance
but certainty.

Luci Shaw

The Dove
Genesis 8:12
John 1:32

Twice sent to signal
God's relenting,
my flights were short
but to the mark.

I lighted first on land
and then on light:
the flood of grace
the grace of blood.

I saw both times
His mercy spent,
Christ buy what God
could not redeem.

John Leax

Jordan River

Naaman went down seven times.
Imagine it—the skin coming
clear & soft & the heart too.
But can you vision clean Jesus
under Jordan? John Baptist did,
holding the thin pale body down,
seeing it muddied as any sinner's
against river bottom, grimed
by the ground of his being.

Rising then, he surfaced, a sudden
fountain. But who would have expected
that thunderclap, the explosion of
light as the sky fell, joining itself
to him, violent, gentle, a whirr of
winged pieces witnessing his work,
his worth, shaking him until the drops
flew from his shoulders, wet & common
& holy, to sprinkle the Baptizer.

Luci Shaw

Tempted
Mark 1:12-13

Still wet behind the ears, he's Spirit-pushed
up Jordan's banks into the wilderness.
Angels hover praying 'round his head.
Animals couch against his knees and ankles
intuiting a better master. The Man
in the middle—new Adam in old Eden—
is up against it, matched with the ancient
Adversary. For forty days and nights
he tests the baptismal blessing and proves to his dismay
    the Man is made of sterner stuff than Adam:
    the Man will choose to be the Son God made him.

Eugene H. Peterson

A metaphor made of bread & stones

*". . . what man is there of you, who, if his son shall ask him for a loaf,
will give him a stone. . . ?"*
Matthew 6:9

*"And the tempter came and said unto him, If thou art the Son of God,
command that these stones become bread. But he answered and said,
It is written, Man shall not live by bread alone, but by every word
that proceedeth out of the mouth of God."*
Matthew 4:3, 4

I stopped in a field the township owns
To watch some heavy roadside stones
Rising into loaves of snow,
A wonder bread baked slowly at
A Fahrenheit of four below
And given away in these few words
To the empty winter eye, quite free,
As it was given unto me.

Jene Beardsley

The water turned to wine

Man become manna
Word become water
Flesh of the willing
Food for the weak

Woman at well
Could not find her bridegroom.
Wedded to five and wenched by another,
She was parched and alone,
Athirst for true love.

Man become manna
Word become water
Flesh of the willing
Food for the weak

Woman at well
Found water for living.
Here was a banquet too good to pass over.
Her bridegroom himself
Was the Caterer's spread.

Man become manna
Word become water
Flesh of the willing
Food for the weak

"Feast on my flesh,
Drink of my lifeblood.
Water that's drunk from wounds that are bleeding,
Is the wine of rejoicing
For heaven's new bride!"

Barbara K. Olson

"Other seeds fell into good soil"
Mark 4:1-20

The soil, moist, dark, a bed for conception,
receives the seed. Soon new life
is kicking in the belly of Mother Earth.
Salvation's age-old shape repeats

Christ lines in these children fathered
by the man-making seed of a prodigal God.
And not a bastard in the bunch.
"Phylogeny recapitulates ontogeny!"

In the background faithful farmers keep
a pentecostal hearth-fire,
stir a sacramental pot of soup
as harvest hands stream in to supper.

Eugene H. Peterson

"Take heart, it is I: have no fear"
Mark 6:45-52

Equally at home
   in the eremitic hills,
   on the corybantic waves,

this modest messiah
   with his quiet commands
   neither rants nor raves.

From a pool of silence
   at the base of solitude
   he lifts a law that saves:

storm-stilling sentences
   coruscating peace
   in a million naves.

Eugene H. Peterson

Uprising
Luke 5:17-26

I was lowered to Him
Who came down to me.
That hole in the roof
Is proof of difficult descent,
As friends with frenzied hands
Tore tiles right and left
And cleft the crowd with dangling cot,
That I might not be forgot
In all that press of pride and misery.

He looked down at me
And saw all that I had been,
And probed the sin that brought me there.
Despair of soul smote sore upon
His tender heart—and for my part
I trembled lest He make me well
And toll the knell of all the ills
That covered me—for suddenly
My sickly cloak was ripped aside
And pride lay prostrate at His feet.

He would not heal by my desire;
He had to raise the man entire,
Or not at all.
And the rising was to me
More fearful than the fall.
The hole of desperation
Where I had entered
Fain would now have been my exit.
But His words blocked all escape
Except the door:
"Be your sins forgiven." And the rape
Of all that bound me to the floor
Was painfully complete; I rose,
His outstretched hands to meet.

Elton D. Higgs

The loss
Matthew 5:30

Because it offended me,
I lopped off my right hand
and dropped it behind me
into the shadowy noplace
where the Adversary is said to lurk

It fell as a root
and burrowed thumb-first
into the blind field,
sprouting fine white tendrils

Its chill blossom, a crown of fingers,
wavers in my sleep,
the petals cold and blue

I pluck that bloom for candles,
lighting them with a knife
dipped in blood and water

The light they shed is a web of shadows,
on which that severed hand lurches,
a maimed spider,
dribbling behind it a thread of regret

Better to lose that crabbed part
than to find at the end
my whole body grown to a stalk of weed
to be plucked up and burnt,
a candle of desire burning itself to naught

Eugene Warren

"Before Abraham was born, I Am."
John 8:58

"I am . . ."?
What? You are what?
King? Counselor? Shepherd? Prince?

Everyone is something.
A doctor is a healer.
A lawyer is a defender of truth.
A merchant is a dealer in fine goods.
But You. "I am . . ."? What?

It's incomplete.
King Henry the. . . .
A man for all. . . .
A penny for your. . . .

Please.
It's unnerving.
Unkind.
Very nearly insulting.
As though no words
quite fit.
It's so huge.
It's so high.
It's so

Mark R. Littleton

The sighting
for Megs & David Singer
John 9

Out of the shame of spittle,
the scratch of dirt,
he made an anointing.

Oh, it was an agony—the gravel
in the eye, the rude slime, the brittle
clay caked on the lid.

But with the hurt
light came leaping; in the shock & shine,
abstracts took flesh & flew;

winged words like view & space,
shape & shade & green & sky,
bird & horizon & sun,

turned real in a man's eye.
Thus was truth given a face
& dark dispelled & healing done.

Luci Shaw

Breaking blindness
John 9:1-41

This body, servant to a begging bowl,
   battered in marketplace bustle,
has toughened to the taunts,
   has turned to stone.

Whose sin enclosed him in the hollows of his bones
   he knows not.
His hopes have learned to focus only
   on the slowly turning now:
      a coin, thudding on the ground,
      gruel for his bowl,
      sleeping straw for when the silence falls.

"Who sinned that he has come to this?"
   "Who sinned?" "Who sinned?"
The words buzz but do not sting
   him who long since stopped the dream of seeing.

The feel of hands upon his face.
A touch that is not rude bumping.
A word that is not a taunt:

"Neither this man nor his parents sinned."

A first light, tender like a violet,
crawls through a hair-breadth chink of stone.

The voice that says, "Go to the pool, wash
   the mud from your eyes,"
falls like oil
   on long-forgotten wounds.

Liquid streams from his face, each drop
   a new found spark,
     a flash of light.

The mud breaks open in a stream of light and water.

He who was born blind sees.

In the marketplace, rude bustle,
   harsh words,
     taunts,
       hardness.
He sees his fellow beings:
A whole generation of stones,
   tumbling in the dark,
     blind to the one who sees.

Ruth El Saffar

Ordinary loaves and fishes

At night I lie beside my child and sing.
Last night I sang "Great Is Thy Faithfulness."
Her back was pressed against my chest,
and the smell of wind was in her hair.
Before I'd finished singing she was sleeping,
but I sang on softly of your faithfulness,
faithfulness that made you pursue your people
even after the green of Eden faded.
At first you came in cloud, in fire,
feeding, leading, sealing
covenants with rainbows, oaths with flames
that passed at dusk between halves of heifer,
ram and goat. Your raw presence was too much for men.

Then, when time was right, you
who were cloud and flame came closer,
and the glory that before could not be looked upon
settled on your son, asleep in a woman's arms.
And in him men saw that the God who fathered them
longed for them, loved them.
There were thirsty deserts, waffling followers.
Yet, faithful to your love for men,
he went your way, another son following father
to the stony place of sacrifice.
This time though, no ram in thicket,
no staying of the father's hand.

And now, as your strange ways would have it,
the Spirit that is you has come to me
and I, not ark, bear you through the world.
Bearer of your image, I? I do no miracles—
make no manna, sight no blind eyes.
I tie laces, make beds, bake bread.
But your equations, like your ways, are strange

adding oil, multiplying meal, making one lunch
food for thousands. Take my acts,
ordinary loaves and fishes.
Bless, break, multiply.

Sanna Anderson Baker

The endless remnant
Luke 9:10-17

"We Lord? What have we to give these people,
Breadless and thirsty, tired and far from home?
Barely enough for ourselves we brought,
Spent from our journey of power,
Where demons obeyed, and your Good News
Was spread to every town about.
And yet you ask us now to serve
This mob with the remnant of our bread?"

"What know you of what is left
From the measure of power I gave?
The Kingdom of God was storehouse for
Your dusty journey of mercy to
Village after village of those in need.
You took no purse, but drew on credit
From Heaven itself. When made you
Tally of where God's bounty stops?"

Then Jesus took the loaves and fish
And gave them up to God,
While people sat to see what Heaven would send.
All ate, and to the dusty remnant found no end.
Twelve baskets full of scraps were then
No more, nor less, than loaves and fish had been.

Elton D. Higgs

The good Samaritan

"A certain Samaritan, who was on a journey, came upon him, and when he saw him, he felt compassion. . . . and bandaged his wounds."
Luke 10:33-34

Compassion.

The stoop of a listening father.

The touch and wink
of a passing nurse.

The gnarled fingers
of a grandmother
steadying a swing.

The clench of a surgeon's teeth
as he begins his cut.

The open hand and pocketbook
of a traveling Samaritan.

The dew of heaven
on dry lips.

Mark R. Littleton

The unmerciful servant

"Summoning him, his lord said, 'You wicked slave, I forgave you all
that debt because you entreated me. Should you not also have had
mercy on your fellow slave, even as I had mercy on you?'"
Matthew 18:32-33

Mercy flows
from the springs of God
like blood from a mortal wound.
It blooms upon earth
like a flush
on a quiet woman's cheek.
It takes root and grows
when exposed to light and Son.
It is only when men take it
and hoard it,
that, like manna the day after,
it rots and stinks.

Mark R. Littleton

The Father
Luke 15:11-32

Never had the old man made such a journey.
His robes enfolded him like driving wind.
No one remembered the old man running. Even fire
had never moved him. His estates were the light
of the town. Yet, there he was, running to a dark
figure huddling the road. Love was flood-water

carrying him forward. Some tried to dike the water;
nothing could hold him. Love loosed a wind
of words: "My son is coming home." Dark
grief behind, the father ran, arms open as light.
He had to lift the boy before his son's fire
of sorrow burned the father's sandals. Journey?

The old man could remember no other journey
but this homecoming: he held his son in the fire
of his arms, remembering his birth: water
and fire. Servants ran along thrusting at the wind
of excitement: what shall we do? what torchlight
prepare? "Bathe away the pig-pen-slopping-dark

that cloaks my son. Prepare a banquet. Jewel the dark
with fires. My son was dead. My son is afire
with life. The land is fruitful. Joy is its water.
Where is my eldest son? The end of the journey
is ours. My son, do you grieve? turn from the light
to say you are unrewarded? Son, is the wind

from the south closer than you to me? Is the wind
of your doubt stronger than my love for you? Water
your hardness, my son. Be a brother to the dark
of your brother's sorrow. Be a season of light
to his coming home. You will make many a journey
through cities, up mountains, over abysses of fire,

but for tonight and tomorrow, my eldest, fire
your heart, strike at its stone. Let it journey
toward dawning, be a thrust at the dark
your brother will never forget. Find a woman of water
and fire, seed her with sons for my name and wind-
supple daughters for bearing daughters and sons of light.

I am a father of journeys. I remind you the dark
can be conquered by love-blazing fire. I made air and wind
a compassionate homeland. Be at home in the light."

Sister Maura Eichner

A meditation

"I am the vine, ye are the branches: He that abideth in me, and I in him, the same bringeth forth much fruit: for without me ye can do nothing."
John 15:5

Much fruit;
You, the vine:
What does it mean?
Many poems? Many souls
gathered to God; so,
the white fields
harvested?

Or—
Fruit fairly glows
on a table:
health, freshness,
peach lushness escape
confinement of wood—
and a silver bowl is
glossed by red.
These gifts? This
setting?

Or—
Do I bear an image?
Cézanne's apples, cherries,
intense, global:
fruit captured,
inspirited; a still life
spills over.
Closer?

Some, but more
elemental,
processional,
and sound:
a branch, pruned,
exposed to light—
splintered, bright—
and a blossom,
down;
your true nature, mine:
espousal:
wholeness
ripening you,
your sphere, orchard without end
thus—then
blessed
disciple.

Sandra R. Duguid

He who would be great among you

You whose birth broke all the
social & biological rules—
son of the poor who accepted
the worship due a king—
child prodigy debating with
the Temple Th.D.s—you
were the kind who used
a new math
to multiply bread, fish, faith.
You practiced a
radical sociology:
rehabilitated con men &
call girls. You valued women
& other minority groups.
A G.P., you specialized in
heart transplants.
Creator, healer,
shepherd, innovator,
story-teller, weather-maker,
botanist, alchemist,
exorcist, iconoclast,
seeker, seer, motive-sifter,
you were always beyond,
above us. Ahead
of your time, & ours.

And we would like
to be *like* you. Bold
as Boanerges, we hear ourselves
demand: "Admit us
to your avant-garde.
Grant us degree
in all the liberal arts
of heaven."

Why our belligerence?
Why does this whiff of fame
and greatness smell so sweet?
Why must we compete
to be first? Have we forgotten
how you took, simply, cool water
and a towel for our feet?

Luci Shaw

Upper room

Stars sing, light-years deep in silent space.
In a bottle's neck God's Ghost sings
as the wine is poured.
Out on the edge of eternity, the Father
sees the Lamb slain ere the world is formed.
A soft cough splits the silence of this room
light-years below the wheeling stars.
A hollow prayer; give it breath, O Ghost,
let roar a wind like that which shook
the bones in Vision Vale.
For vision, God spills bread crumbs on the board.
His stars sing, light-years deep in silent space.
Here, emblems speak a mystery of brokenness:
the shattering of him by whom all things consist.

Keith Patman

The sureness of this hour

The blandness of His body
still in my mouth,
the commemoration of His blood
cupped in my hands,
I pause in prayer.

Beside me my daughter,
too young to know
the verses that she knows,
draws a man
with a heart-shaped head.

She tells me it is me.
The sureness of this hour
is reconciliation.
The bread, the blood, her love
confound my double nature.

John Leax

from Bloodcount II

How well chosen wine was
to stain our souls with remembrance!
He knew how it burst, vivid,
from the flushed skins of grapes
grown for this sacramental crushing:
a shocking red, unforgettable as blood
a rich brew in the cup, a bitter,
burning in the throat, a warmth within,
chosen well to etch our lintels
with the paradoxes of
a high priest bound to his own altar,
death as a tool of love,
and blood as a bleach.

Luci Shaw

Christographia 2

In the center, the Bread, enthron'd
in a silver dish
  (a shallow boat gliding
  to the breaking

& the Wine, casting blood-shadows
as the light sings thru it)
calls me   reflections form a single
intense star in the center of
the brimming glass

within the Bread, the shine
of the sun's rising
flames, its hurricane spindles
spelling our each and nova names

thus, calld
thus, answerd

sought & found
in one, uncleavable act

we are bound each to each
through the Center
Who only *is,* imaged now in what
we chew taste sip swallow;
flesh to flesh, a commitment
and enactment of joy

this Bread carries our wounds,
& this Wine's wet with pain
we ownd (once: now we own One
Who gives us ourselves)

the Voice dances from
throat to throat, granting us
song, in our measure,
& joy without measure or reserve

yet if I try to preserve the moment
it turns worm in closed palm:
He leads, swiftly, He leads, surely, He leads

Eugene Warren

At Communion

Whether I kneel or stand or sit in prayer
I am not caught in time nor held in space,
But, thrust beyond this posture, I am where
Time and eternity are face to face;
Infinity and space meet in this place
Where crossbar and upright hold the One
In agony and in all Love's embrace.
The power in helplessness which was begun
When all the brilliance of the flaming sun
Contained itself in the small confines of a child
Now comes to me in this strange action done
In mystery. Break time, break space, O wild
And lovely power. Break me: thus am I dead,
Am resurrected now in wine and bread.

Madeleine L'Engle

All these breads

all these breads—
matzo, rye,
tortillas, soft indian disks,
unbleached wheat—
broken, torn, snapped, crumbs
floating down from soft loaves
or popping up from the sheets
of perforated matzo—
these many grains
grown in red soils, black loam,
grey or yellow clay,
roots of wheat and oats
and barley and rye
probing dirt & rain,
the slender, parallel-veind leaves
arching in sun or lying
straightend in a strong wind—
crusht, ground, rolld, sifted
at last becoming
all these breads–
one diverse loaf passing
from hand to hand,
dying into each mouth,
sprouting a new
& shining grain

Eugene Warren

Two stanzas: the Eucharist

Annie Dillard speaks of Christ
corked in a bottle: carrying the wine
to communion in a pack on her back
she feels him lambent, lighting
her hidden valleys through the spaces
between her ribs. Nor can we
contain him in a cup. He is always
poured out for our congregation.
& see how he spills, hot, light,
his oceans glowing like wine
flooding all the fjords among
the bones of our continents.

Annie Dillard once asked: How
in the world can we *remember* God?
(Death forgets and we all die.)
But truly, reminders are God's
business. He will see to it,
flashing his hinder parts, now,
then, past our cut in the rock.
His metaphors are many, among them
the provided feast by which
our teeth & tongues & throats
hint to our hearts of God's body,
giving us the why of incarnation,
the how of remembrance.

Luci Shaw

Banquet song

Why is the weight of this white sacrament
So great today upon my tongue? The mass
Is white and light. Christ's body is not meant
To burden and oppress. Yet I confess
A heaviness of words beneath the weight.
I am constrained into a speechlessness
And the dumb terror of too much too late
Of knowledge. Heavy master, bless and press
My tongue into a slower quietude,
Hold it from talk, touch it, train it to taste
The beaten body and the sauce of blood.
So will my arteries sing in the waste
Of any Gobi, and green leaves ascend
From red oases where I ate my friend.

Chad Walsh

"Is it I?"
Mark 14:17-21

Christ's round-table seminar
on sin, with wine
   and bread for a snack,
for a moment
   strays
from the psalm (was it the fifty-first?) they
   are studying together
and gets personal.
   Ideas
   in the head
are realized
as facts in the heart.
Tympanic questions
   percuss
   the drumhead table:
Is it I/Is it I/Is it I?
Will I be among the lucky
   eleven? Or will
I be the luckless
   one?
Will doubt tonight mature in my denial?
Will sloth
   sleep out a final betrayal?
Will greed break out
   and make its grab?
Kyrie eleison. Kyrie eleison.

Eugene H. Peterson

Judas, Peter

because we are all
betrayers, taking
silver and eating
body and blood and asking
(guilty) is it I and hearing
him say yes
it would be simple for us all
to rush out
and hang ourselves

but if we find grace
to cry and wait
after the voice of morning
has crowed in our ears
clearly enough
to break our hearts
he will be there
to ask us each again
do you love me

Luci Shaw

Cock-crowing

"And the Lord turned and looked at Peter. And Peter remembered the Lord's words . . ."
Luke 22:61

Grey dawn
Gone
But day
Still waits.
Cock-crowing
Flowing
Flashing
Tearing
Through anguished heart.
Part
Of me
Is dead—
The thread
Of boasting, knowing,
Throwing words about—
Is snapped,
And dangling ends ensnare the dawn.

Dark my heart since dawn
And dark the curtain drawn
Across my soul
By fear which stole
My light away.
But day must come.
The One Who prophesied the broken thread
And gazed on new made shreds
Can knit my soul and turn
Cock's call to Light indeed.
It needs my Master's face
To make cock-crowing
Both breaking
And making
Of dawn's first rays.

Elton D. Higgs

Birth trauma
Mark 14:51-52

   Pushed
from the Hebrew-Hellenic womb
   running scared
into the Roman night

   naked
as a newborn

afterbirth of old righteousness
   on the pavement

were you, Mark, embarrassed
   to lose your shirt?
   satisfied to save your life?

Eugene H. Peterson

Royalty

He was a plain man
and learned no latin

Having left all gold behind
he dealt out peace
to all us wild men
and the weather

He ate fish, bread,
country wine and God's will

Dust sandalled his feet

He wore purple only once
and that was an irony

Luci Shaw

The blessing
*Blessed are the peacemakers,
for they shall be called sons of God*

Making peace
requires action

sometimes crossing the street
when the light is red

swimming upstream
getting bruised

maybe dying

Jean Janzen

The Revolutionary

Do you
wince when you hear his name
made vanity?

What if you were not so safe
sheltered, circled by love
and convention?
What if
the world shouted at you?
Could you take the string
of hoarse words—glutton,
wino, devil, crazy
man, agitator, bastard,
nigger-lover, rebel,
and hang the grimy ornament
around your neck
and answer
love?

See the sharp stones poised
against your head! even
your dear friend
couples your name with curses
("By God! I know not God!")
the obscene affirmation
of infidelity
echoes, insistent,
from a henhouse roof.
Then—Slap! Spit! the whip,
the thorn. The gravel
grinds your fallen knees
under a whole world's weight
until

the hammering home of all
your innocence
stakes you, stranded
halfway between hilltop and heaven
(neither will have you).

And will you whisper
forgive?

Luci Shaw

Weeknights at the Cathedral

Weekday evenings, I watch you
stuff soprano into boy
into choir robe
like ricotta into a shell,
faces bursting on the high A.
A priest wraps the rotten notes
about his collar,
fingers them like a rosary
till they rise, whole, smooth,
beyond the organ pipes.
Sometimes you hide in those pipes,
pop out on middle C.
Sometimes you filter through the stained glass,
jiggling the tinted cross
till your thorns slip.
Today, hunchbacked on the fourth pew,
canvassed in greys,
you kneel, a beggar woman.
I think you are praying for me.

Marjorie Maddox Phifer

How to decorate an egg Ukrainian style

As you etch the design onto the egg,
divide the sphere evenly.
Imagine lines from pole to pole and equatorial;
imagine stretching a rubber band around the tips
then draw the banding lines.
You may etch with pencil or with razor blade.
You'll want to count the cost.
Hold the egg gingerly, fingertip pressure—
the way eye contact draws and holds a glance;
the way you work to hover a balance beam;
never clenched, and not the luxury
of a fistful of egg.

As you draw, remember the season,
the body broken for you,
the table of devotion which began as blood,
the way of pain in love.

Placing a cross anywhere means sacrifice.
This one, on an eggshell,
may take a life before it can be drawn or dyed.
Choose your symbols thoughtfully—
the fish, the grapes,
the line that circles without ending or beginning.
Your hand may tremble; it's difficult to conceive
the idea of forever, even on an egg.

The dyeing seems the simple part.
You work from light to darkest colors
then you block out with beeswax what you want to keep.
Isn't it often just the way?
Stepping toward darknesses;
having to let the past and the present die;
having to cover all that you treasure
while you try to imagine the outcome.
The more detailed you choose to be,
the more of the egg will be blackened by wax.
How much are you willing to dye?

Last is the melting, removing the wax by heat,
but not too hot or too fast,
or you'll end up holding the yolk.
Unintentional scrambled anything is hard to retrieve.

After the wax melts off, you'll see what you did.
You'll find that the longer you work,
the fewer surprises there are of design.
And you'll be able to do more intricate things.
Of course, the more you're given,
the more will be required.
That really is the way of love,
of anything that promises renewal.

Nancy Nase Thomas

Foresight
1 Peter 1:18-21

Before lambs bled in Egypt, One was given.
Before the worm tore Eden, pain was faced.
Somewhere, before earth's cornerstone was placed,
a hammer crashed in heaven—nails were driven.

Keith Patman

Flesh become Word

On the way to becoming Word,
he remembered hands:
the planning, piecing together bones,
sketching creases on palms.
And hands, pointing, naming
azalea, edelweiss, rose;
hands shadowing eyes,
hands stained with soil.
He remembered the midwives' hands
tugging Boaz, Solomon, Joram into light,
and his own: fingers translucent in the womb.
For a moment, he again mixed clay,
beckoned children,
drew letters in sand,
until the hammer struck again.

Marjorie Maddox Phifer

Cross

I dreamed it was a baby
just shriveled from the womb,
eyes filmy,
a baby whose bird-like bones stretched
just beyond the crossbeam
and no further,
a baby who forgot to scream
at the hammer's thud,
thought the sharp nail a nipple,
sucked the world in.

Marjorie Maddox Phifer

Craftsman

Carpenter's son, carpenter's son,
is the wood fine
and smoothly sanded, or rough-grained,
lying along your back? Was it well-planed?
Did they use
a plumbline
when they set you up? Is the angle true?
Why did they choose
that dark, expensive stain
to gloss the timbers
next to your feet and fingers? You
should know, You who,
Joseph-trained, judged all trees
for special service.

Carpenter's son, carpenter's son,
were the nails new and cleanly driven
when the dark hammers sang?
Is the earth warped from where you hang,
high enough for a
world view?

Carpenter's son, carpenter's son,
was it a job well done?

Luci Shaw

Reminder
Mark 15:21-32

My key-ring keeps the design of redemption
pendant from my ignition and,
when I'm walking, repeats the sound
of nails noisily in my pocket.

The same bloodsoaked timbers that signed
the worst of deaths, pinning a spreadeagled
Christ to the sky, are used in my town
for life-raft Fonts and picnic Tables.

Death, not Christ, changed meaning when Christ
and cross were joined. Murder was a catalyst
for mercy. And so my metal ring
sings its small hymn in cadence with my heart.

Eugene H. Peterson

Hands

You hold us
In your hands
Yet put yourself,
Oh foolish Lord,
In ours.

The more fools, we
Who nail the hands
That hold us
To a tree.

Elizabeth Rooney

Hurting

Only pierced hands
Are gentle enough
To touch some wounds.
The quivering flesh
Shrinks even from love,
Yet knows
That without this touch
There can be no healing.
How can one reach
A deeply hidden hurt
Without revealing
A massiveness of pain
That makes the helper
Cringe in dismay?
You need
To have been crucified yourself
If you would find the tenderness
To stay and share the pain
Again and yet again.

Elizabeth Rooney

"Why hast thou forsaken me?"
Psalm 22:1

Perhaps the Socrates he had never read,
The Socrates that Socrates poorly understood,
Had the answer. From opposites, opposites
Are generated. Cold to heat, heat to cold,
Life to death, and death to life. Perhaps the grave's
Obscenity is the womb, the only one
For the glorified body. It may be
Darkness alone, darkness, black and mute,
Void of God and a human smile, filled
With hateful laughter, dirty jokes, rattling dice,
Can empty the living room of all color
So that the chromatic slide of salvation
Fully possesses the bright screen of vision.

Or perhaps, being man, it was simply
He must first go wherever man had been,
To whatever caves of loneliness, whatever
Caverns of no light, deep damp darkness,
Dripping walls of the spirit, man has known.

I have called to God and heard no answer,
I have seen the thick curtain drop, and sunlight die;
My voice has echoed back, a foolish voice,
The prayer restored intact to its silly source.
I have walked in darkness, he hung in it.
In all of my mines of night, he was there first;
In whatever dead tunnel I am lost, he finds me.
My God, my God, why hast thou forsaken me?
From his perfect darkness a voice says, I have not.

Chad Walsh

To a friend dying on Good Friday

You also are in agony.
The uncertainty is breaking my heart.
I am thinking—with Him
there was no anguish of awaiting the outcome;
death was sure. The end
was known from the beginning.
It was only a matter of time,
and even that was quick enough.

But for you it is different.
Three o'clock does not come
and I am not sure about your Easter morning.
I don't know what to hope.
I hardly dare to breathe
and I cannot stand beneath your cross
and let you see me
crying with the others.

It is unknowing that is anguish.
The spirit has no resting place,
no end, however terrible, to shore against.
Perhaps that is why He,
human, in that darkness,
wept and sweated in the Garden,
cried out from the cross.
It was uncertainty.

Myrna Reid Grant

Lines after Herbert: Rondel

The contrarieties crush me. These crosse actions
Do winde a rope about, and cut my heart.
Good deeds are turned to sudden malefactions.
The end was never guessed at in the start.

How these stern contradictions break apart
The simplest words, and purest actions.
The contrarieties crush me: these crosse factions
Do winde a rope about and cut my heart.

A fearsome faith provides the only cautions.
O dear my Father, ease my smart.
Reality permits of no abstractions.
The whole is visioned in each broken part.
The contrarieties crush me: the crosse's actions
Do winde a rope about and hold my heart.

Madeleine L'Engle

Lovingkindness 1 & 2

God's strong arm
extends to selfish bullies, willful, crude;
endures the self-deceived; ignores the rude;
forbears with murder; incest does not quell.
And when my arm would sweep them all to hell,
His little finger draws them to his heart.

God's strong arm
in love applies the rod, employs the lash;
impairs a face; in beauty strikes a gash;
denies the hungry; wounds a nursing breast.
And while I raise my fist, beseech, protest,
His thumb imprints a poem with the pain.

Beverly Butrin Fields

Tapestry for a reliquary of the True Cross

This is the warp—call it colorless
and the weft:
                        silk wound with silver
for the angels' wings,
rose, olive, iridescence like the hummingbird's
but permanent.
                        Saints in the highest—
richly coruscating in the light of Christ
and of myriad burial candles—
                                    sing too.
Out of their mouths sounds rise to circling
gulls of sin
                cranes for watchfulness:
                                            two birds.
Two of the Marys stay, attentive.
They are lifting his forsaken body
from its nails.
                    John has taken his new mother
home to weep. This is the time for it.
Earth shuddering
                        and the split veil
                        and his side.
A perfect blood-of-Jesus red so spills
the restraint of God,
                            while in the lower
left-hand corner, woven in, your face
looks on,
                find it? Hands open to enclose
each drop; tongue swallows in remembrance.
You have no idea what the thought of Jesus
renders now,
                    inexhaustible and
unseen as cross threads.

Susan Bergman

Expectation

"All they that see me laugh me to scorn: they shoot out the lip, they shake the head, saying, He trusted on the Lord that he would deliver him: let him deliver him, seeing he delighted in him."
Psalm 22:7-8

"Show us a miracle," we said.
The double pair of nail-holes bled.
The rose of thorn-pricks ringed his head.

"Show us a miracle," we pleaded,
And almost feared. Suppose God heeded
Our giggling plea, and interceded?

The ninth hour came. No God appeared.
He hung there limp and neatly speared.
Why should a helpless God be feared?

Chad Walsh

Taking flesh

". . . save yourself! Come down from the cross, if you are the Son of God!"
Matthew 27:40

This is the saving, this pain
this not coming down
this tearing of the veins
by my own weight
this breaking.

It is here that I feel
the meaning of this body's need,
the flesh, so heavy, so tender,
so hard to lift away from,
huddling against me in trembling fear,
knowing that my deepest dream
is leaving it.

I could not go home
without this knowing.
In the anguish of my body's cry
the very sky is torn.
My Father's face breaks through.
I shall not die.
We shall not die.

Ruth El Saffar

Dead and buried

And so we took him down
(Or thought we did),
Wiped off the sweat and spittle
From his face,
Washed the dried blood,
Threw out the crown of thorns,
And wrapped him once again
In swaddling clothes.

A tomb can be a cramped,
Confining place,
Far smaller than a stable.
We laid him there
(Or thought we did).
We were not able
To comprehend
The infinite contained.
For us, it was the end.
Only the harsh realities
Of death and stone
Remained.

Elizabeth Rooney

Re-enactment

"I'm so frightened," she gasped as she ran through the open door,
   Her face nearly pale as death,
And then held to my shoulders as though she might drop to the
      floor
   If she could not catch some breath.

"What is it?" I said as we both sank onto a chair,
   Still grasping each others' arms.
I was gripped by a nameless dread that filled the still air,
   As though knowing her cause of alarm.

"I can't tell you," she said, "what came over me just now—
   I was only trying to fix . . ."
And, trembling, pointed at her palm to show:
   "He fell off . . . the crucifix."

"And with hammer and nails you tried to replace Him there,"
   I said, and suddenly knew,
As I spoke, the horror she'd felt the minute before,
   Of flesh with nails driven through.

We sat still, each estranged to ourselves, yet each knowing our
      guilt
   For the first time. I lowered my head
And, "Forgive me," she sighed, "for the wounds and the pain You
      felt,
   For I knew not what I did."

She quietly left, and I rose to take Him down
   From the wall where He filled the whole room,
Replaced the cross on its nail, then gently wrapped Him,
   Unsure where to make His tomb.

Cynthia Walkwitz

Easter Saturday

A curiously empty day,
As if the world's life
Had gone underground.
The April sun
Warming dry grass
Makes pale spring promises
But nothing comes to pass.

Anger
Relaxes into despair
As we remember our helplessness,
Remember him hanging there.
We have purchased the spices
But they must wait for tomorrow.
We shall keep today
For emptiness
And sorrow.

Elizabeth Rooney

Plain fact

The winter cold
has not yet left my bones.
I shiver in this birthing Spring's
first light.
No sun, no shadow,
only the truth
of tree and slated sky.
Though no bird sings,
with certitude I brace
against the failing chill,
awaiting Easter.

Myrna Reid Grant

I believe in the Resurrection

What chance at apostleship have I,
mouthing the Creed, buried deep
in blankets, dreading the day.
I clutch the dark, the sweet
oblivion of sleep, its cushioned coma.
Dawn nudges night,
finding stones and dispensing orders
while I cling to my crypt
as though I hadn't heard
where the power is, or that death wishes
are doomed, or that day's
determined light
will raise me, wide-eyed.

Barbara Esch Shisler

Poem for Easter

Rise, daffodil,
against the stones
that shall yield
to your yellow vow.

Rise, onion shoot,
from an odious shroud
to green exclamation;
your death is done!

Rise, children
of the winter mind,
run to the garden—
kneel to the sun.

Barbara Esch Shisler

Quickening

Dead trees draw life
when the days expand and the sun
fulfills its promise, oft delayed
by the clutch of ice.

Clotted, gnarled, knotted twigs
on the trees sense sap and the death
of death. They stretch, begin
to puff green on the end.

Men sing new songs
of a Life laid down for rebirth
when Easter is the Spring
and the branch is Christ.

Mark A. Noll

Rib cage

Jonah, you
and I were both signs
to unbelievers.

Learning the anatomy
of ships and sea animals the hard way—
from inside
out—you counted (bumping your stubborn head)
the wooden beams and curving bones
and left your own heart unexplored.
And you were tough.
Twice, damp but undigested
you were vomited. For you
it was the only
way out.

No, you wouldn't die.
Not even burial softened you
and, free of the dark sea prisons,
you were still
caged in yourself—trapped
in your own hard continuing rage
at me and Nineveh.

For three nights
and three days dark as night—
as dark as yours—
I too charted the innards
of the earth, swam
in its skeleton, its raw under
ground. A captive
in the belly of the world
(prepared, like the fish, by God)
I felt the slow pulse at the monster's heart,

tapped its deep arteries, wrestled
its root sinews, was bruised
by the undersides of all
its cold bony stones.

Submerged,
I had to die, I had
to give in to it, I had
to go all the way
down
before I could be freed,
to live
for you and Nineveh.

Luci Shaw

Et Resurrexit Tertia Die
(Bach, *Credo*, B-minor Mass)

Three short days of twilight and darkness,
dawn and the light. The elements, free
of all knowledge, unblessed by prediction, yet sensed the
    suspense—
Creator entombed by creation, the loftiest heights
brought low, the universe madly askew. Three
short days with the length of three endless nights.

Three times, forced by its nature to shine
the sun reluctantly rose. In the skies no sign
through clouds of a bow. The earth which knew not how sinless
its Maker turned Captive had been yet felt the wrong.
The winds whistled dirges. Three endless
days—then the groan of creation exploded in song.

Mark A. Noll

Ode: entropy & Easter

that all things wear out, break down,
erode, crack, shatter,
sag, splinter, break;

due to neglect
the rooftree gives way—
and there is no way
to avoid neglect
something is always left undone
something always overlooked

if we knew when
the thief would come,
cancer grow,
the bombs fall,
we could take reasonable precautions
but we work against night and decay
with little light,
and in ignorance of the next moment

the seed must die to grow
and yet our life—
scripture says it—
is as brief and tenuous
as the wild flower trembling
in every breeze, scorched
by the sun, clipped
by the frost

all things run down to dust at last,
they crumble and scatter, are lost
the wind chimes clatter
against Rose's sung alleluia,
the guitar's throbbing chords,
as I reach with ink

for an affirmation, seeking
a light seeded and rooted
beyond—beneath—above
the light that is only sun

how easy to say
"he is risen, it is Easter at last
and darkness has lost"—
yes but harder to say lightly
against the weight
of a body riddled with cancer,
of a child tortured and murdered
of the twist of the spine
that makes walking a cacophony

Easter can be true only
if the Cross was truly
the death of God
and Man in one body—
sung alleluias flower
only from that dark root
of final disaster
when all seeming hope is lost—
then can the dead rise—
and praise be alive at last

Eugene Warren

Mary

The Love I love
Came in the early dawning
Standing as still as light.

How could I ever have dreamed
So sweet a morning
After so dark a night?

Elizabeth Rooney

Easter morning, yesterday

A lily shivered
at His passing,
supposing Him to be
the Gardener

Margaret D. Smith

Opening

Now is the shining fabric of our day
Torn open, flung apart, rent wide by love.
Never again the tight, enclosing sky,
The blue bowl or the star-illumined tent.
We are laid open to infinity
For Easter love has burst His tomb and ours.
Now nothing shelters us from God's desire—
Not flesh, not sky, not stars, not even sin.
Now glory waits so He can enter in.
Now does the dance begin.

Elizabeth Rooney

Christographia 31

Christ came juggling from the tomb,
flipping and bouncing death's stone pages,
tossing those narrow letters high
against the roots of dawn spread in cloud.
This Jesus, clown, came dancing
in the dust of Judea, each slapping step
a new blossom spiked with joy.

Hey! Listen—that chuckle in the dark,
that clean blast of laughter behind—
Christ comes juggling our tombs,
tossing them high and higher yet,
until they hit the sun and break open
and we fall out, dancing and juggling
our griefs like sizzling balls of light.

Eugene Warren

Christ's crown

The leaves emerge—a growing
garland lying lightly on his head.
The dance of Spring, of resurrection,
quicks his feet; from all directions
caper those he'll call his own.
The sun shines warming down upon
the dancers and their pivot. Only those
up close can smell and see the thick
black-red the flowers nurse upon.

Mark A. Noll

Seed

God dug his seed
into dry dark earth.
After a pushing up
in hopeful birth
and healing bloom
and garland grace
he buried it again
in a darker place

Twice rudely-planted seed,
root, rise in me
and grow your green again,
your fruited tree

Luci Shaw

Festival
"There shall come forth a shoot from the stump of Jesse, and a branch shall grow out of his roots."
Isaiah 11:1

Jesse's roots, composted with carcasses
of dove and lamb, parchments of ox and goat,
centuries of dried up prayers and bloody
sacrifice, now bear me gospel fruit.

    David's branch, fed on kosher soil
    blossoms a messianic flower, and then
    ripens into a kingdom crop, conserving
    the fragrance and warmth of spring for winter use.

Holy Spirit, shake our family tree;
release your ripened fruit to our outstretched arms.

    I'd like to see my children sink their teeth
    into promised land pomegranates

And canaan grapes, bushel gifts of God,
while I skip a grace rope to a Christ tune.

Eugene H. Peterson

The comfort of rocks

The comfort
of rocks

their condensed
stability

like our spirits
at peace

like all my weight
in resignation

leaning on a boulder
in the field

fiddleneck
nodding beside

a cabbage butterfly
floating

from cup
to cup

Christ unwrapping
his graveclothes

slipping through
the tight molecules

and sitting down
to eat with me

Jean Janzen

Easter magic

Had we crucified the rabbit—

yanked him from his fields of grass
and staked him out by paws and tender feet
to quiver, twitch and die in agony
of innocence,
and then, in three days' time,
had seen him hop up from the tomb
unscathed
but for the wounded paws and feet we felt—

then maybe now we'd talk of Christ,
pass his story down from child to child
and only faintly hint at silly myths of
wicker baskets,
chocolate eggs,
treasures hidden in the field
and some trick hare who died

then somehow disappeared.

Leslie Leyland Fields

To know him risen

Is it obliquely
   through time's telescope, thick-
   lensed with two thousand Easters?
Or to my ear in Latin, three chanted
   'Kyries' triumphing over a purple chancel?
Or in a rectangular glance at sepia snapshots
   of Jerusalem's Historic Sites?
Can I touch him through the cliché crust
   of lilies, stained glass, sunrise services?
Is a symbol soluble?
Can I flush out my eyes and rinse away
   the scales?
Must I be there?
Must I feel his freshness
   at an interval of inches? and sense, in-
   credulous, the reassurance of warm breath?
   and hear again the grit of stone
   under his sandal sole?
   those familiar Judean vowels
   in the deep voicing of beatitude? recognize
   the straight stance, quick eye,
   strength, purpose, movement, clear command—
   all the swift three-day antonyms of death
   that spring up to dispel its sting,
   to contradict its loss?
Must I be Thomas—belligerent in doubt,
   hesitant, tentative, convinced, humbled, loved,
   and *there?*
Must sight sustain belief?
Or is a closer blessedness
   to know him risen—now
   in this moment's finger-thrust of faith—here
   as an inner eyelid lifts?

Luci Shaw

Wounded

You could feel its edges.
You could run your fingers over its red lips
   and probe the hollow like a mouth.
In a way it had been a thing of beauty;
   the steel, so sharply bright,
   sliding cleanly between the layers,
   slicing the sheets of cells,
   the turfed flesh folding back
   bringing the blinding white and red
   into that land of pulsing gloom.

Thomas, you are like me;
   our faith begins in fingering
   the open wounds.
It is as if our hopes cannot spring free
   save by permission of those hands,
   that side; as if only after all
   our doubts turn tail—shadows
   before light and blood—
   can the words "My Lord, my God!"
   burst from our mouths
   as wide as wounds.

John Shaw

"Thou art he that took me out of the womb."
Psalm 22:9

I will sing a new song unto the Lord.
His glory has not worthily been spoken
Though every leafy tree and blade of grass
Whispers in wind to tell his hidden Name
And though the chipmunk, charged with sun and
   air,
Descends into his temple under earth

To say his prayers of praise. O choirs of earth—
Leaf, scale, feather, fur, hair—proclaim the Lord!
Set in movement the molecules of air.
Let the secret word openly be spoken,
Let the high echoes answer back the Name,
And breath of angels furrow through the grass.

Though he has made me fleeting as the grass,
Though mole and I are shaped of brother earth
And to the earth return—O praise his Name,
All things that breed and die. Know he is Lord
Of the amino acids, and the word spoken
To dust raised Adam's eye into the air.

For thou hast lifted me into the air
A little while, to tread the patient grass
With moving weight, and hear thy word spoken—
Eden, Sinai, the ends of any earth,
The cross into the skull. Speak the word, Lord,
The private word into my heart: thy Name.

O speak it now, and speak my hidden name
Planted in thee before birds broke the air.
Say who I am and introduce my Lord.
Ye little lives that nestle in the grass,
Slim creatures underground, wings above earth,
Be silent quickly, for the Lord has spoken.

Be clamorous quickly, for the Lord has spoken.
Sing in polyphony his public Name,
Descended out of heaven to the earth.
Say, sing, chant the Name of Jesus in air
Kissing with Easter green the risen grass
That is the emerald carpet of the Lord.

The risen Lord has looked at me and spoken.
Though I am grass, he calls me by a name.
Sing high, bright air; praise him, brothers of earth.

Chad Walsh

Open

Doubt padlocked one door and
Memory put her back to the other.
Still the damp draught seeped in
though Fear chinked all the cracks and
Blindness boarded up the window.
In the darkness that was left
Defeat crouched in his cold corner.

Then Jesus came
(all the doors being shut)
and stood among them.

Luci Shaw

Easter for five senses

He lives! Is living! Moves free before us,
released now from torn bonds of clay and of clay,
bright sun for our warming, bright sun for our seeing,
burning the shrouds of our blindness away.

This genesis odor, this fragrance of living,
deathstench dispensed with the linens left there.
No need for wrapping with spice to preserve this,
no need for aloes to perfume the air.

This wine, newly poured, this vine (we the branches),
this seed sown, corrupted, to living restored,
this food of his giving, this struck rock stream welling,
this "come, taste and see," this bread from His board.

This warmth of torn flesh to our finger (and hand) thrust,
this honey comb, fish proof for those who might question,
this walk shoulder to shoulder expounding the scriptures,
at dusk at our table, this hand-lifted blessing.

These murmurs of "peace" for ears stopt with weeping,
love's syllables shining from this O loved voice,
this new in a newness evoking new lyrics,
new melodies brimming with praises. Rejoice!

Marie J. Post

Companion

When first He joined us, coming, it seemed, from nowhere,
and yet, somehow, as if he had followed us a long, long time,
immediately, He was one of us, no stranger, but
a close companion, speaking softly, familiar with our lives,
these days, the answers to our doubts.

And when we moved Him to at least partake of food,
He stood there at the table, not as guest, but host,
and broke the bread to portions, one for each,
then poured the wine, His dark-marked hands
blessing the wine and us. Was it that act,

His broken hands raised up against the wooden walls,
the prayer-bowed head, the gently spoken word
or some reflection trembling in the wine,
a thickening of air, a luminosity not of wavering light,
that pierced our hearts with joy,

that filled our mouths with praise? O praise!
O joy! Then suddenly the light withdrawn,
no longer form and lifted hands above the bread.
Stumbling, we found the road to town,
knowing that never, never would we walk alone again.

Marie J. Post

Galilee outing

The widening space between our usual mooring
and our small skiff shows us at last adrift.
A few hours here can work their wonders, curing
anxieties, perplexities that sift,
that have been sifting, buzzing, moving
unanswered over us—a cloud of bees.
Here in remembered peace, a proving
of answers given may bring our worn hearts ease.

Buoys mark the shallows, gently tolling.
A wind comes up to ease our task, to fill the sail.
With early morning come sounds of water rolling
against the shore and, in the dawn's first pale,
soft light, one beckons, with arms spread
in welcome, to faith's fire, to fish and bread.

Marie J. Post

Christographia 21

Vicit agnus noster.

signs above, signs below,
the burning earth, the bleeding sea,
the locust armies, the dying stars;

see angels stand on sea & land,
hear thunders trumpet, mountains crumble,
taste the ashes of Babel's smoke;

taste the wind from the darkened sun,
hear the mouths on the Beast's horns,
see the Dragon devour men;

the locust armies, the dying stars,
the burning earth, the bleeding sea,
signs above, signs below.

signs above, signs below,
the natal star, the joyous tomb,
Herod's terror, the scatterd sheep;

see the sun grow dark at noon,
hear the song of newborn stones,
taste the bread that Heaven bakes;

taste the wine of the only vine,
hear holy silence praise the Word,
see the Lamb who dying lives;

Herod's terror, the scatterd sheep,
the natal star, the joyous tomb,
signs above, signs below.

Eugene Warren

The partaking
John 6:53-56

Bread of the Presence
was
in Moses' day
served on engraved gold plates
to you and your select few.
And in exclusive glory
one alone and lonely man
sprinkled, with fear,
the ceremonial drops that pleaded
failure for another year
to you, known then
as only high and holy—
heavens apart
from common men.

Often we taste the
granular body of wheat
(Think of the Grain that died!)
and swallow together
the grape's warm bitter blood
(Remember First Fruit!)
knowing ourselves a part of you
as you took part
of us, flowed
in our kind of veins
quickened cells like ours
into a human subdividing.

Now you are multiplied—
we are your fingers and your feet,
your tender heart—
we are your broken side.

Take now and crumble small and
cast us
on the world's waters—
your contemporary shewbread.
Feed us
to more than five thousand men
and in our dark daily flood of living
pour yourself out again!

Luci Shaw

The way the leaf falls

In the garden a child
testing God's will:
the way the leaf falls
will answer yes or no.
Remembering I laugh
and lift my arms
to trees—all leaves
are yes,
their bold unfoldings
and their layered
patience
secrets
trembling in the dusk,
all the falling
coins
    crowns
        flames
            yes.

Jean Janzen

Evergreen

topped
with an earth-bound angel
burdened
with man-made stars
tinsel bound
but touched with
no true gold
cropped
girdled with electricity
why be
a temporary tree
glass-fruited
dry
de-rooted?

when you may be
planted with purpose
in a flowered field
and where
living in clean light
strong air
crowned with the repeated gold
of every evening,
every night
real stars may nest
in your elbow
rest
be found in your shade
healing
in your perennial green
and from deep springs your roots
may suck enough to swell
your nine sweet fruits

Luci Shaw

Christographia 14

Is it chance
or dance moves
the world?
Grooves of matter
habited to change,
a strange clatter
of dark atoms—
or living light,
a bright park
Adam's stricken
heirs all lost?

Is the world
blind and dumb
or bloom, festal?
A vain jest,
or holy feast?

The Christ answers,
dancers are stars,
sharers all in
music's space;
He is calling
in the fallen partners.
We're the weight
His leaping heart bears.
In great peace
the stately sport fares
through the spirit
that dares rejoice.

Eugene Warren

The foolishness of God
for Gerald Hawthorne
1 Cor. 1:20-25

Perform impossibilities
or perish. Thrust out now
the unseasonal ripe figs
among your leaves. Expect
the mountain to be moved.
Hate parents, friends and all
materiality. Love every enemy.
Forgive more times than seventy-
seven. Camel-like, squeeze by
into the kingdom through
the needle's eye. All fear quell.
Hack off your hand, or else,
unbloodied, go to hell.

Thus the divine unreason.
Despairing now, you cry
with earthy logic—How?
And I, your God, reply:
Leap from your weedy shallows.
Dive into the moving water.
Eyeless, learn to see
truly. Find in my folly your
true sanity. Then, Spirit-driven,
run on my narrow way, sure
as a child. Probe, hold
my unhealed hand, and
bloody, enter heaven.

Luci Shaw

The tree

The children say the tree must reach the ceiling,
And so it does, angel on topmost branch,
Candy canes and golden globes and silver chains,
Trumpets that toot, and birds with feathered tails.
Each year we say, each year we fully mean:
"This is the loveliest tree of all." This tree
Bedecked with love and tinsel reaches heaven.
A pagan throwback may have brought it here
Into our room, and yet these decked-out boughs
Can represent those other trees, the one
Through which we fell in pride, when Eve forgot
That freedom is man's freedom to obey
And to adore, not to replace the light
With disobedient darkness and self-will.
On Twelfth Night when we strip the tree
And see its branches bare and winter cold
Outside the comfortable room, the tree
Is then the tree on which all darkness hanged,
Completing the betrayal that began
With that first stolen fruit. And then, O God,
This is the tree that Simon bore uphill,
This is the tree that held all love and life.
Forgive us, Lord, forgive us for that tree.
But now, still decked, adorned, in joy arrayed
For these great days of Christmas thanks and song,
This is the tree that lights our faltering way,
For when man's first and proud rebellious act
Had reached its nadir on that hill of skulls
These shining, glimmering boughs remind us that
The knowledge that we stole was freely given
And we were sent the Spirit's radiant strength

That we might know all things. We grasp for truth
And lose it till it comes to us by love.
The glory of Lebanon shines on this Christmas tree,
The tree of life that opens wide the gates.
The children say the tree must reach the ceiling,
And so it does: for me the tree has grown so high
It pierces through the vast and star-filled sky.

Madeleine L'Engle

The Poets

Sanna Anderson Baker graduated from Wheaton College and the program for Writers at the University of Illinois at Chicago. She teaches writing at Wheaton College and mothers three daughters.

Jene Beardsley says: "I was born and raised just outside of New York City. Receiving my B.A. in English literature from Wheaton College in 1958, I went on to earn my M.A. in the same subject from the University of Illinois in 1959. In that year I began teaching English at Eastern College in St. Davids, Pennsylvania, where I have continued through the present. I have a son, two daughters, and a grand-daughter. My home is King of Prussia, Pennsylvania."

Susan Bergman lives in Lake Forest, Illinois and is currently teaching art history at Trinity College, Deerfield. After attending Wheaton College she lived in several cities, including New York, where she helped edit a literary magazine and studied poetry. Two children help to keep her occupied.

Kelli Conlin says: "After graduating from Saint Mary's College in Notre Dame, Indiana, I went on to obtain a Masters Degree in Journalism from Northwestern University. Aside from poetry, I have a serious dedication to photography, in which I am involved in my work for *Outside Magazine.*"

David Craig was born in Berea, Ohio in 1951. He has a B.A. from Cleveland State University, and an M.A. from Colorado State University. He is the author of *The Sandaled Foot* (Cleveland State University Press) and *Psalms* (My First Press). He is currently working as a cab driver.

Sandra R. Duguid teaches English at Northeastern Bible College in Essex Fells, New Jersey. She has conducted numerous classes in Creative Writing, has taught in the N.Y.S. "Poetry in the Schools" program, and was a tutor in poetry at the St. David Christian Writers' Conference. She is listed in *A Directory of American Poets,* and was elected to the Poetry Society of America in 1982. Her work has appeared in poetry anthologies such as *The Country of the Risen King,* and in magazines such as *Sojourners, Anglican Theological Review,* and *West Branch.* She and her husband, Henry Gerstman, live in West Caldwell, New Jersey.

Sister Maura Eichner is a prolific poet who is teaching English at the College of Notre Dame of Maryland. Her work has appeared in

Commonweal, The New York Times, Poetry, The Sewannee Review, and many other journals, and has been recorded for the Poetry Collections at Harvard University and the Library of Congress. She has received several awards for distinguished teaching, and is the author of the books *What We Women Know* (Sparrow Press) and *A Word, A Tree: Christmas Poems* (Franciscan Graphics).

Ruth El Saffar is a University Research Professor of Spanish Literature at the University of Illinois, Chicago, and lives in River Forest, Illinois, with her husband and three children. She holds workshops for community groups on techniques for stimulating the creative imagination.

Beverly Butrin Fields says: "I have a B.A. in English and have begun work on an M.A. in linguistics. Recently I lived in Israel for a year studying Modern Hebrew. My husband, two small children, and I spend summers in Alaska, involved in commercial fishing. My poems have been printed in *Arkenstone, Eternity, Christianity Today, Christian Educators Journal,* and *The Banner.*"

Leslie Leyland Fields received her B.A. from Cedarville College, Ohio, in 1979, and in 1984 her M.A. in Journalism from the University of Oregon where she is now completing an M.A. in English. She lives in Alaska (when not in school) where she participates in a family commercial fishing operation.

Myrna Reid Grant, on the graduate communications faculty of Wheaton College, is also a book and scriptwriter. She travels frequently to the United Kingdom, Europe, and Third World countries. She has four children and lives in Wheaton, Illinois.

Elton D. Higgs is professor of English at the University of Michigan at Dearborn. Born in Abilene, Texas, in 1937, he attended Abilene Christian College, the University of Washington, and the University of Pittsburgh. He is married, with two children.

Jean Janzen lives in Fresno, California. She graduated from Fresno Pacific College, and received her M.A. in English (Creative Writing) at California State University, Fresno. Wife of a pediatrician, mother of four, she has discovered in mid-life some of the possibilities and joys of language. Her poems have appeared in magazines such as the *Christian Century* and the *Christian Leader.*

Lisa Leafstrand, a Wheaton College graduate, has had her poetry published in *Mademoiselle, Atlantic Review,* and other magazines, and is the winner of a Hopwood Award in Poetry from the University of Michigan, where she received an M.A. in English. She is an editor of children's books in New York City.

John Leax is poet in residence at Houghton College. His books include *Reaching into Silence, In Season and Out: A Steward's Journal,* and *The Task of Adam.*

Madeleine L'Engle has written over thirty books, including *A Wrinkle in Time,* for which she received the Newbery Medal in 1964, and *A Swiftly Tilting Planet* which received the National Book Award. The Regina Medal was given her in 1983 for her contribution to children's literature. A book of her poetry, *The Weather of the Heart* (Harold Shaw) was published in 1978. She is Librarian and writer in residence at The Cathedral Church of St. John the Divine and travels widely to lecture and lead retreats. She and her actor husband, Hugh, live in Crosswicks, their Connecticut home, when they are not in New York City.

C. S. Lewis is almost universally known as one of the great thinkers of our century. Born in Ireland in 1898, he taught at both Oxford and Cambridge and is best known for his Christian apologetics as found in volumes such as the *Abolition of Man,* and *Mere Christianity.* He was also a scholar, fiction writer, literary critic, and superb essayist. He died in 1963 but his ideas live on in a concise and beautiful form in his poetry. The brief poem in this collection is taken from his collected *Poems.*

Mark R. Littleton is a graduate of Colgate University (1972) and Dallas Theological Seminary (1977). He has worked as a youth pastor and is presently in industry in Hunt Valley, Maryland. His poetry has appeared in many journals including *His, Christianity Today, Moody Monthly, Eternity, Contemporary Christian,* and *The Other Side.*

Joe McClatchey says: "My academic interests can be summed up as Story and Worship. I hold degrees from Bob Jones University, The Southwest Christian Seminary, and Arizona State University. Since 1970 I have taught English at Wheaton College, specializing in Victorian literature, The Inklings, classical mythology, and Arthurian romance." His poems have appeared in magazines such as the *Cresset,* and *Christianity Today.*

Beth Merizon is a free-lance writer living in Grand Rapids, Michigan. A graduate of Calvin College, she formerly worked as an editor and journalist for Christian Schools International.

Mark A. Noll, who is married and has two children, teaches history at Wheaton College and does research on Christianity in America. Among his favorite authors are John Calvin, Edmund Crispin, P. D. James, Martin Luther, Edmund S. Morgan, and J. R. R. Tolkien.

Barbara K. Olson teaches high school English at Minnehaha Academy in Minneapolis, Minnesota. Her own education includes a B.A. and an M.A. in English from Wheaton College and the University of Minnesota, respectively, and graduate study at Trinity Evangelical Divinity School. She loves choral music, baseball, and deep dish pizza.

Keith Patman, a native of Washington, D. C., has a B.A. in English from Bryan College. He and several other Bryan alumni published *Arkenstone* magazine from 1976-1981. For the past seven years Keith and his wife, Frankie, have lived in Asheville, North Carolina, where he taught English, art, and drama at Ben Lippen School. The Patmans are now training as linguists with Wycliffe Bible Translators. They have a daughter, Lauren, born in 1983.

Eugene H. Peterson says: "My essential work as a person and as a pastor oscillates between the poles of Scripture and prayer, the revealed word and our answering words, the capital Word become flesh, and our words becoming flesh. Making a poem, for me, is a way of joining discipline and playfulness, in being attentive both ways to words and to where words come from." Peterson is the pastor of Christ our King United Presbyterian Church, U.S.A., in Bel Air, Maryland, and the author of *A Slow and Certain Light,* and *Run with the Horses* (both InterVarsity Press).

Marjorie Maddox Phifer, a Wheaton College graduate, teaches Creative Writing and Composition at the University of Louisville where she is completing her M.A. in creative writing. She has received several inter-university poetry awards, and has published poetry in numerous journals and magazines, including *Alchemy, Confrontation, His, Louisville Review, River City Review, Sanskrit, Wellspring,* and others.

Marie J. Post is a graduate of Calvin College, and has taught Junior High School. She has written poetry for the Grand Rapids Press for 25 years, and her book *I Had Never Visited an Artist Before* was published by Being Publications. Her verse has appeared in many magazines and journals and also takes the form of hymns.

Elizabeth Rooney began writing poetry in 1978 after joining the Society of the Companions of the Holy Cross. She and her husband, an Episcopal priest, operate the Cave of the Mounds in Blue Mounds, Wisconsin. She is one of the ten Christian women featured in *Bright Legacy* (Servant Publications).

John Shaw, a Wheaton College graduate, recently received his M.D. from the Stritch School of Medicine at Loyola University. As well as writing poetry, he is enthusiastic about photography, calligraphy, cartooning, and singing with the guitar. Presently in the U.S. Navy, he hopes in future to practice medicine in a Third World country.

Luci Shaw grew up in England, Australia, and Canada and graduated from Wheaton College. She is Senior Editor at Harold Shaw Publishers in Wheaton, and lectures on poetry, imagination, and creativity at many colleges and writers' workshops. In the cracks of her life she writes poems, and her three books of verse are *Listen to the Green, The Secret Trees,* and *The Sighting*. Her work has appeared in several anthologies and literature text books as well as many magazines. She and her husband Harold have five children and three grandchildren.

Barbara Esch Shisler is a Mennonite poet whose work has appeared in secular and religious journals. Two chapbooks of her work were published by Pinch Penny Press of Goshen College. She lives in Pennsylvania with her husband, has three grown children, and works part-time at Provident Bookstore.

Margaret D. Smith writes poetry, short stories, and articles. After graduating in 1980 from Seattle Pacific University she was a newspaper reporter and taught poetry to children as well as adults. She and her family live in Juneau, Alaska, near a swiftly-calving glacier.

Nancy Nase Thomas received a B.A. from Wheaton and an M.A. from Villanova University. She says: "Words, the teaching of writing, and attempts to give ideas incarnate form have haunted me always. A precious family, two growing children, and the love of music and friends have formed the lively and painful matrix in which my poems have taken shape. At present I teach part-time in the English Department at Eastern College, St. Davids, Pennsylvania."

Cynthia Walkwitz is a 1981 graduate of Wheaton College, where she divided her time among writing, gymnastics, dance, and occasional studying. For the past two years she has taught gymnastics and dance in Nashville, Tennessee. She hopes to put her writing ability to work full-time in Christian ministries.

Chad Walsh, an Episcopal priest and retired teacher (Beloit College) is the author of six books of poetry and various works on literature and religion. His book of poems on Psalm 22, *The Psalm of Christ,* was published in 1982 (Harold Shaw). He is the father of four daughters and has eight grandchildren. At present he is writing a book composed of "interviews" in which the characters will share their memories of Jesus.

Eugene Warren was born in Colorado in 1941. He grew up on a farm in Eastern Kansas. He teaches English at the University of Missouri—Rolla. Married for twenty-one years, he has four children. He is the author of several books, including *Geometries of Light* (Harold Shaw).

Acknowledgements

Abelard Schuman, New York, for "Banquet song," and "A quintina of crosses," by Chad Walsh, from *The Unknowing Dance,* © 1964 Abelard Schuman.

Arkenstone, for "During Communion," by Keith Patman.

The Banner, for "Companion," "Easter for five senses," and "Galilee outing," by Marie J. Post.

Christian Century, for "The comfort of rocks," and "The way the leaf falls," by Jean Janzen, © 1982 Christian Century Foundation. Reprinted by permission from the November, 1982 issue.

Christian Leader, for "Christmas program," and "The blessing," by Jean Janzen.

Christianity Today, for "Lovingkindness 1 & 2," by Beverly Butrin Fields; "Quickening," by Mark A. Noll; and "Is it I?" by Eugene H. Peterson.

Colorado Quarterly, for "The sureness of this hour," by John Leax.

Cresset, for "Breaking blindness," and "First parting," by Ruth El Saffar; "The Father," by Sister Maura Eichner; and "Who was also himself looking for the kingdom of God," by Joe McClatchey.

Franconia Conference News, for "Poem for Easter," by Barbara Esch Shisler.

Harcourt, Brace, Jovanovich, Inc., for "The Nativity," from *Poems,* by C. S. Lewis, © 1964 by The Executors of the Estate of C. S. Lewis. Reprinted by permission of the publisher.

Harold Shaw Publishers for "The Dove," from *Reaching into Silence,* © 1974 by John Leax; "After Annunciation," "At Communion," "Like every newborn," "Lines after Herbert: Rondel," "O Sapientia," "O Simplicitas," and "Tree at Christmas," from *The Weather of the Heart,* by Madeleine L'Engle, © 1978 Crosswicks; "Bloodcount II," "Chance," "Evergreen," "for who can endure the day of his coming. . . ?" "Made flesh," "Mary's song," "Night's lodging," "Open!" "The partaking," "The revolutionary," "Rib cage," "Royalty," "Seed," "Shine in the dark I, II, & III," "To know him risen," and "too much to ask," from *Listen to the Green,* © 1971 by Luci Shaw; "Craftsman," "The groundhog," and "He who would be great among you," from *The Secret Trees,* © 1976 by Luci Shaw; "the foolishness of God," "Jordan River," "Judas, Peter," "The sighting," "Star song," "Triad: Skull Hill," and "Two stanzas: the Eucharist," from *The Sighting,* © 1981 by Luci Shaw; "Expectation," "Thou art he that took me out of my mother's womb," "Thou didst make me hope upon my mother's breasts," and "Why hast thou forsaken me?" from *The Psalm of Christ,* © 1982 by Chad Walsh; "All these breads," "The loss," and "Ode: entropy & Easter," from *Geometries of Light,* © 1982 by Eugene Warren.

His, for "Christ's crown," by Mark A. Noll; "Away in a manger," by Barbara K. Olson; and "Some Christmas stars," by Luci Shaw.

Ktaadn Molehill Pamphlets, for "Christographia 19," by Eugene Warren.

Mission, for "Cock-crowing," "The endless remnant," and "The Uprising," by Elton D. Higgs.

The Other Side, for "I believe in the Resurrection," by Barbara Esch Shisler.

Rejoice! for "Prayer at the Advent log," by Jean Janzen.

Still Point Press, for "Judah's Lion," and "Snow," from *Star Like a Lion's Eye,* © 1980 by Keith Patman.

Thinker: a Literary Journal, for "God tries on skin," by Marjorie Maddox Phifer.

Time of Singing, for "Hewn Hands," by David Craig.

Grateful acknowledgment is also made to all the poets who permitted the inclusion of their previously unpublished poems in this anthology.

other books in the **Wheaton Literary Series:**

The Achievement of C. S. Lewis, by Thomas Howard. "Written with Lewis's own passionate power with words."—*Peter Kreeft.* Paper, 196 pages

And It Was Good: Reflections on Beginnings, by Madeleine L'Engle. Vivid personal reflections on the character of the Creator and his creation. Cloth, 219 pages

Creation in Christ: Unspoken Sermons, by George MacDonald, edited by Rolland Hein. Devotional essays revealing a deeply moving understanding of holiness and man's relationship to God. Paper, 342 pages

Geometries of Light, poems by Eugene Warren. "He shows how abundantly love has poured Itself into our 'seed-filled light' and 'night-locked flesh.'"—*Robert Siegel.* Paper, 108 pages

A Guide Through Narnia, by Martha C. Sammons. A detailed study of Lewis and his Chronicles of Narnia, with map, chronology, and index of names and places. Paper, 165 pages

Images of Salvation in the Fiction of C. S. Lewis, by Clyde S. Kilby. Explores the Christian meaning in Lewis's juvenile and adult fiction. Cloth, 140 pages

Life Essential: The Hope of the Gospel, by George MacDonald, edited by Rolland Hein. "A book for those who hunger after righteousness."—*Corbin S. Carnell.* Paper, 102 pages

Listen to the Green, poems by Luci Shaw. Poems that see through nature and human nature to God. Illustrated with photographs. Paper, 93 pages

The Miracles of Our Lord, by George MacDonald, edited by Rolland Hein. "A better set of meditations on the miracles of Christ would be hard to find."—*Walter Elwell.* Paper, 170 pages

The Psalm of Christ: Forty Poems on the Twenty-second Psalm, by Chad Walsh. Diverse and powerful poetry from a highly acclaimed poet. Paper, 74 pages

The Secret Trees, poems by Luci Shaw. "These are the real thing, true poems . . . they work by magic."—*Calvin Linton.* Cloth, 79 pages

The Sighting, poems by Luci Shaw. "Few poets in our day can speak of incarnational reality with the eloquence of Luci Shaw."—*Harold Fickett.* Paper, illustrated with photographs, 96 pages

Tolkien and The Silmarillion, by Clyde S. Kilby. A fascinating view of Tolkien as a scholar, writer, creator, and Christian, based on Kilby's close association during the collation of The Silmarillion. Cloth, 89 pages

Walking on Water: Reflections on Faith & Art, by Madeleine L'Engle. Shows us the impact of the Word on words and ourselves as co-creators with God. Cloth, 198 pages

The Weather of the Heart, poems by Madeleine L'Engle. "Read her poetry and be chastened and filled with joy."—*Thomas Howard.* Cloth, 96 pages

The World of George MacDonald: Selections from His Words of Fiction, edited by Rolland Hein. "A treasure of a book—one to be read and reread."—*Frank E. Gaebelein.* Paper, 199 pages

Available from your local bookstore, or from HAROLD SHAW PUBLISHERS, Box 567, Wheaton, Ill. 60189